This Walker book belongs to:

_____

_____

First published 1991 in *Greek Myths*
by Walker Books Ltd, 87 Vauxhall Walk, London SE11 5HJ

This edition published 2017

2 4 6 8 10 9 7 5 3 1

© 1991, 2006, 2017 Marcia Williams

The right of Marcia Williams to be identified as author/illustrator of this work
has been asserted by her in accordance with the Copyright, Designs and Patents Act 1988

This book has been typeset in Goudy Old Style

Printed and bound in Great Britain by Clays Ltd, St Ives plc

British Library Cataloguing in Publication Data:
a catalogue record for this book is available from the British Library

ISBN 978-1-4063-7158-1

www.walker.co.uk

Pandora's Box
— & —
Perseus and the Gorgon's Head

Marcia Williams

WALKER BOOKS
AND SUBSIDIARIES
LONDON · BOSTON · SYDNEY · AUCKLAND

Contents

Pandora's Box

Perseus and the Gorgon's Head

Pandora's Box

Chapter One
The Birth of Mankind

Long ago in Ancient Greece, the gods lived a heavenly life at the top of Mount Olympus, way above the clouds. The chief of these gods was Zeus, who was as wild as the winter storms. He was quick to anger and loved to fill the sky with thunderbolts!

Zeus was afraid of nothing and no one, except perhaps his wife, Hera. Hera was exceptionally beautiful, but she was sharp-tongued and vengeful. Luckily for him, Zeus could hide from her by changing into any animal he liked, so she didn't often get the better of him.

When Zeus was in a good mood, Mount Olympus was a delightful place for the gods. They had an easy life, with very little work to do and every day they dined together on ambrosia brought to them by doves. This honey-flavoured delight gave the gods the gift of immortality.

"Well, we're so heavenly," Zeus was often heard to say, "that the world would fall apart without us. We've got to go on for ever, like it or not – and I like it – so pass the ambrosia!"

***

Down on earth there lived a race of giant gods called Titans. The Titans were lesser gods, so they weren't allowed to live on Mount Olympus, but most of them had magical powers and they were all incredibly strong! Sadly, apart from each other, their only companions were the wild beasts, which roared around their feet.

"Beasts are fine for hunting and eating, but you really can't have a decent conversation with a lion," moaned Prometheus, one of the Titans.

"I find crocodiles charming company, as long as you avoid their teeth," replied his brother, Epimetheus.

"You always were an idiot," complained Prometheus. "No wonder I'm lonely!"

"Who are you calling an idiot?" muttered Epimetheus.

"Actually," Prometheus continued, ignoring his brother completely, "I think I shall make some companions out of clay – at least they wouldn't talk rubbish!"

"No, they won't talk at all – even I can tell you that," Epimetheus mumbled to himself.

Prometheus was cleverer than the other giants and a good potter besides, so he carried on regardless and made some tiny clay people.

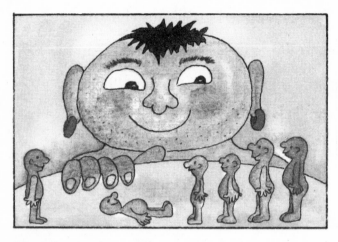

They looked just like miniature Titans and when Prometheus looked down on them, he chuckled with delight.

"My little dolls!" he cried. "Let us pass the time together – I can share all my great knowledge with you."

But his little friends made no answer.

"It matters not," said Prometheus, "I love you anyway, and today I shall tell you the colours of the rainbow."

The days passed and Prometheus began to tire of talking to his silent companions, so he shouted up to Mount Olympus, "Hey, Zeus!" he yelled. "Can you puff a bit of life into this little lot?"

Zeus looked down from his high throne and sighed, "You are a very demanding giant. One day you will test my patience too far!"

However, he was in a good mood that day, and much to Prometheus's delight he breathed life into the little clay people. Humankind was born.

Chapter Two
Prometheus Plays a Trick

Prometheus loved his people and his people loved him. Their days were full of wonder and delight and Prometheus saw to it that they were free of all troubles and ills. Over time, Prometheus's people multiplied and their numbers grew. He taught them everything he knew. (Which for some of them was a little too much!)

"We love you, Prometheus," one child said. "But do we really need to know all this stuff?"

"Well," Prometheus replied, "as you're never going to be as bright as me … probably not. But I will teach you the most important thing – respect for the gods!"

"Of course, Prometheus," they chorused. "We'll always respect the gods, even the lesser ones, like you!"

"Especially the lesser ones like me," grumbled Prometheus. "Zeus is not the only one with a brain, whatever he may think! Even so," he continued, "you must keep on his good side by making the odd sacrifice.

"Oh we will," one man cried. "I sacrificed

two hens and a cow just last week."

"No wonder there were all those thunderbolts flying around," laughed another. "I heard that Zeus is a vegetarian!"

"Stop joking and listen – this is important," said Prometheus. "It is not enough to make a sacrifice, you have to do it according to Zeus's rules or there'll be trouble."

At that very moment Zeus sent a thunderbolt hurtling to earth just to remind mankind of his power – which it did.

Harmony reigned between humankind and the gods until, in a moment of boredom, Prometheus decided to play a trick on Zeus.

Confused as to how to offer a sacrificial cow to Zeus, some of the men asked Prometheus to show them what to do.

"Where should we put the prime cuts?" one asked. "Should they go in the same bag as the liver and kidneys?"

"Does Zeus like to eat the eyeballs," asked

another, "or should we remove them?"

"Well now," said Prometheus, his eyes glinting, "I think you should do it like this." And he bent down low to divide the cow between two sacks. He placed a big juicy steak on top of the sack of guts and eyeballs, and on top of the other sack, which was full of delicious chops, steaks and other prime cuts, Prometheus piled the cow's guts.

He offered both sacks to Zeus.

"Hey, Zeus," he shouted, offering both sacks up to Mount Olympus. "These kind people have slaughtered a cow for us and divided it into two bags. Which one would you like?"

"Hera, get the pan on. It's steak for tea," cried Zeus gleefully and he sent down his eagle to retrieve the sack with the delicious-looking steak on top.

When Zeus discovered the true contents of the sack, he roared with such fury that the mountain shook and great boulders hurtled down into the valley.

"Call this steak?" he thundered. "It's guts and eyeballs, you rogue!"

"Bad luck, Zeus," laughed Prometheus.

"But I'm sure your doves will arrive with some ambrosia before sunset. I doubt you'll go hungry."

Zeus was beside himself with anger. Thunder and lightning shot across the skies, mountains rumbled and seas roared. Even Hera hid under her throne! Zeus did not like being made a fool of and was determined to have his revenge. Knowing how much Prometheus loved humankind, Zeus extinguished every single flame and

spark of fire on earth. The earth became a
very cold place to be. There was nothing
to light up the nights, no fire to cook food on
and no flames to keep the wild beasts away.

"I hope you and your precious people freeze
to death!" roared Zeus.

"Not raw meat and salad again," the people
sobbed. "Oh Prometheus, how could you do
this to us?"

"Never fear," said Prometheus, who was a
little ashamed of what he had done. "I'll fetch
you some fire."

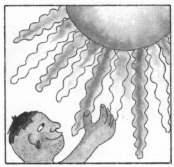

He stole up Mount Olympus and broke off a
blazing piece of the sun. He wrapped it in a
giant fennel leaf and carried it back down to
the people.

"There you go," he said. "Fire! Ouch! Be
careful – it's hot!"

"Three cheers for asbestos fingers!" everyone
shouted as they shared around the flames.

Unfortunately, their joy was short-lived.
Through the clouds came the icy voice of Zeus.
"I'll teach you to mess with me you horrible,
hairy giant!" he roared.

Chapter Three
Zeus Punishes Prometheus

Poor Prometheus had plenty of time for regret – Zeus decided to punish him in the most terrible way. Prometheus was chained to a rock and a great vulture flew down and tore out his liver. This was bad enough in itself, but then every single night, Prometheus's liver would grow back again, so that with each new day, the vulture could feast on a delicious fresh liver.

"I would cook it for you, but we're a little short on fire," said Prometheus to the vulture.

"Bad joke," squawked the great bird. "Sleep's a great healer and I'll be back tomorrow for your new liver."

And so he was. Again and again and again.

Meanwhile, Zeus had not forgotten humankind. He was determined that they should also be punished. He ordered the gods to create a beautiful woman.

"She must be as beautiful as my Hera! Well … almost," he added, hastily.

The gods did their best and it has to be said that their efforts were not bad, for she was indeed beautiful. Zeus was satisfied with their creation and he named the woman Pandora. Zeus called for Hermes, the messenger of the gods, and ordered him to take Pandora down to where Prometheus's brother, Epimetheus, lived.

However, when Hermes knocked on

Epimetheus's door and presented him with Pandora, saying that Zeus had sent him a wife, Epimetheus hesitated. Prometheus had warned him not to accept presents from the gods – but to refuse a gift from Zeus might be very risky indeed.

"Well," Epimetheus said at last, "I had thought I'd be a bachelor for the rest of my life, but if Zeus says you are to be my wife, then I suppose we'd better get on with it. You are certainly very beautiful."

Epimetheus married Pandora the very
next day – and that same day, he regretted it!
Pandora might have been beautiful, but she
was also vain, self-centred and she nagged
him constantly.

"By Zeus, I'm a stunner," she said, as she
preened herself in the mirror. "I can't think
why Zeus didn't marry me himself!"

"Just off hunting, dearest," replied
Epimetheus, who was eager to escape Pandora
for a few hours.

"Bring me back something priceless," she demanded.

"Would a leopard do, dearest?" sighed Epimetheus, rushing for the door.

Then one day, when Epimetheus was out hunting, Pandora found a locked box hidden in his cupboard. She tried to open it, but the lock held it tight shut. When Epimetheus returned from hunting, Pandora was waiting.

"This box, dear heart," she said, "is it full of jewels for me?"

"Oh no, you mustn't touch that," wailed Epimetheus. "It belongs to Prometheus and he expressly said that we weren't to open it."

"Nonsense!" snapped Pandora. "He's chained to a rock! What use has he for jewels? Give me the key. Now!"

Chapter Four
The Box is Opened

For days Epimetheus refused to let Pandora open the box. Each time he went hunting, he would hide it in a new place and take the key with him, but each time Pandora would find it. Try as she might she could not force it open and every time she failed, her longing to open the box grew. Finally, she decided to

steal the box *and* the key while Epimetheus slept.

"Pandora gets what Pandora wants," she whispered to herself, slyly.

One day, when Epimetheus had fallen asleep after a long day's hunting, Pandora stole the box and carefully removed the key from around her husband's neck.

"I told you – Pandora gets what Pandora wants," she smiled as she eagerly fitted the key into the lock. "Oh, I shall soon have more jewels than Hera herself!"

Gently Pandora turned the key and lifted
the lid … the sound of her screams was
terrible to hear for out of the box flew, not
jewels, but every evil and spite imaginable:
anger, sickness, old age, envy and many,
many more. They swarmed out like insects,
covering Pandora and infesting the earth
with pain and sorrow.

Epimetheus, woken by his wife's cries,
rushed to her side and tried to close the lid,
but it was too late, the box was empty.

Only one small and precious thing remained
in the box – hope. Prometheus had hidden
hope amongst all the ills, just in case they

should ever escape. And so Epimetheus sat back and let hope out into the world.

Pandora had done exactly what Zeus wanted. Through her greed, she had brought misery to Prometheus's precious people. When Prometheus was finally released from his rock and heard the news, he was devastated.

"Well," he said, trying to comfort himself and his little companions, "we've still got each other and with hope we can face most things."

Up on Mount Olympus, Zeus was in the best of moods.

"Pass the ambrosia, Hera my love," he grinned. "I think I've meddled with humankind quite enough for now!"

Perseus and the Gorgon's Head

Chapter One
The Twins

Once upon a time, there were twin princes,
Proteus and Acrisius. They lived in a beautiful
palace in the rich and fertile valley of Argos.
Unfortunately, the valley echoed with the
quarrels of the twins, as Proteus and Acrisius
had fought from the day they were born.
They fought over toys, they fought over food,
they fought over pets and they fought over
friends. As they grew older their arguments

grew fiercer and more violent, because they both wanted to be King of Argos. There was no way that either of them would ever agree to share the crown, so each day their quarrelling continued.

"It's my crown!" said Proteus.

"No! Mine!" argued Acrisius.

"Who'd want you for king?" Proteus taunted. "You can't even keep your dog under control, let alone rule Argos!"

"At least I'm not a coward," scoffed Acrisius. "I don't hide under the bed every time my wife loses her temper!"

So the fighting continued, until the day came when Acrisius raised an army and drove Proteus from Argos. Then, he made himself king.

"And if you don't like it," he informed his subjects, "you can go and join Proteus in exile and never, ever see the beautiful valley of Argos again!"

Shortly after King Acrisius's coronation a prophet came to the palace gates, demanding an audience with the king.

"If he brings bad tidings, send him away," ordered King Acrisius.

But the prophet would not leave and insisted on seeing the king to reveal his prophecy.

"For the cruel way you treated your brother," warned the prophet, "you will be most justly punished."

"Take him away," cried the king. "I don't

want to hear."

"Ah, but you will hear what I have to say," continued the prophet, "for it is foretold that your daughter, Danaë, will have a son. A strong and handsome son – who will kill you!"

Having delivered his message, the prophet was dragged away by the guards.

Acrisius turned to his dog, his only real friend. "It's all nonsense, Dog," he declared. "Danaë isn't even pregnant!"

Chapter Two
The Baby Boy

However, not long afterwards his daughter came to him with the happy news that she was indeed expecting a child.

"What!" cried the king. "No way. This can't be. It had better be a girl-child."

For a while King Acrisius thought no more about it, but as the time of the birth came closer, he grew increasingly concerned.

"I'm worried," Acrisius confided to his dog.

"Is the oracle always right?"

"Don't ask me, I'm only a dog," barked the dog.

"Maybe Danaë will have a baby girl and then everything will be all right," smiled the king.

Unfortunately for King Acrisius, Danaë had a baby boy. She named him Perseus, and he was the most beautiful baby anyone had ever seen. Everyone – except for Acrisius and perhaps his dog – was utterly charmed by the infant.

"I told you to have a girl!" shouted Acrisius to his daughter. "Now I will have to get rid of you both."

The very next morning, hard-hearted Acrisius put Danaë and baby Perseus into a wooden chest. He closed the lid, sealing

it tightly, and pushed it out to sea.

"Father," wept his daughter. "Please don't do this. We'll drown!"

"Sorry, but it's for my own good," replied Acrisius, giving the chest an enormous shove.

For the next few days and nights, the wooden chest tossed on the waves. While Perseus slept peacefully in his weeping mother's arms, Danaë was sure that they would drown or else die of starvation. By some miracle, the pair neither drowned nor died; instead, the kind waves washed them up onto the shores of the little Greek island of Seriphos.

Chapter Three
A Proposal Refused

There by lucky chance was Dictys, the brother of the king Polydectes, who was walking along the beach.

"Is this flotsam or jetsam?" puzzled Dictys, peering at the strange chest from which he could hear faint cries.

Curious, he opened the chest and was startled to see a rather bedraggled Danaë and her baby inside.

"Neither flotsam nor jetsam," he laughed, helping Danaë and Perseus out, "but a baby and his mum!"

Realizing that Danaë was no ordinary castaway, Dictys took her to his brother's palace. The grumpy king looked at the pair and grudgingly agreed that they could stay.

So Danaë and Perseus made their home on Seriphos, and Dictys and his wife adopted them as their own.

Perseus grew up to be a strong, handsome young man. He was taller, tougher and cleverer than any other youth in the kingdom. Indeed, he was so quick-witted and strong that many thought he must be the son of a god.

Perseus adored his mother and did all he

could to help her and to protect her. The years
passed and this became increasingly difficult,
as King Polydectes had become obsessed with
Danaë. He thought that he was in love with
her and was determined to marry her, whether
she liked it or not. She despised him but the
more forcefully she refused his advances, the
more determined Polydectes became to marry
her. Soon he could think of very little else and
proposed to Danaë almost every day.

"You are the grape in my wine, Danaë.
You are the most beautiful woman in Greece,"
he wheedled. "For the zillionth time, will you
marry me?"

"No! No! No! No! No!" she replied. "And
again, no!"

"I bet you'd marry me if that drip of a son
wasn't around to protect you," he grumbled.
"I'm going to get rid of him once and for all!"

"I still won't marry you, so there's no point,"

said Danaë, who was terrified of
losing her son.

"If you don't agree to marry me,
I will send Perseus on a deadly
mission, from which he'll never,
ever return!" said the king. "If you
do, I won't – and there's an end of it."

"Send me on your deadly mission," inter-
rupted Perseus, "because I will never, ever let
my mother marry you!"

Chapter Four
A Deadly Mission

So King Polydectes sent Perseus to fetch the head of the terrible Gorgon, Medusa. She was one of three monstrous sisters, with brass hands, golden wings and a gaze that turned men into stone.

Perseus travelled for many days across land and sea in search of the Gorgons, but he could find no sign of them. "I don't know where to look next," he sighed. "I think I'll sleep on it."

Wearily, he lay down to rest and as he slept the goddess Athene, who had heard of his quest, came to visit him. Athene was struck by Perseus's bravery and his beauty.

"What a handsome fellow!" she smiled. "Far too handsome to be turned to stone by Medusa."

Athene woke Perseus and gave him a polished shield in which he could look at Medusa's reflection, so that her ghastly glare would not turn him to stone.

"Remember," she said to Perseus, "whatever you do, only look upon Medusa in the shield."

The next day Perseus set off again, but he still couldn't find any sign of Medusa. When night arrived, Perseus lay down to sleep with his spirits low. As he slept, the god Hermes visited him as he too had heard of Perseus's brave quest.

"Wakey, wakey," whispered Hermes in Perseus's ear, "I have a gift for you."

Hermes gave Perseus a sickle which he could use to cut off Medusa's terrible, snake-covered head.

"It's specifically made for the job," promised Hermes. "But if you want to know how to find Medusa you will have to visit the Grey Ones.

They live over the stream, down the hill,
through the trees and up to the very top of
Atlas Mountain, where you'll find their cave.
Off you go now, no dawdling – the early
Perseus catches the Medusa!"

With a flutter of his winged sandals, Hermes
vanished from sight.

Perseus travelled over the stream, down
the hill, through the trees and up to the very
top of Atlas Mountain where he eventually
reached the Grey Ones' cave. The three sisters

had only one eye and one tooth between them
and as Perseus drew closer he could hear them
quarrelling.

"Give me the eye."

"Who's got it?"

"I can't see. Anyway, I'm hungry so give
me the tooth."

"No, it's my turn for the tooth!" and so on,
without pause.

Silently, sneaking up behind them, Perseus
grabbed both the eye and the tooth.

"What's going on?" they cried. "Who's that?
Give them back! Thief! Thief!"

The Grey Ones screamed in panic, and
Perseus agreed to return their eye and tooth,
but only if they told him where to find Medusa.

"Rot Medusa, I want the eye! Tell him!

Tell him!" cried one.

"Visit the Ocean Nymphs," cackled another. "Now give me the eye and the tooth!"

"No, mine! Give, give!" said the third.

Perseus threw the eye and tooth into their midst and left the three sisters to quarrel amongst themselves.

Perseus climbed back down the mountain until he reached the ocean, where he called

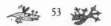

out to the Nymphs.

"Nymphs!" he shouted.

"Who's that battering our eardrums," they cried, rushing to the shore to see.

When the Nymphs heard that Perseus was on a quest to kill Medusa, they were delighted. They hated Medusa and were eager to do all they could to help Perseus.

"What a joy!" they cried. "Kill Medusa? Oh how splendid! We'll certainly help!"

The Nymphs gave Perseus winged sandals

so that he could fly, a helmet to make him invisible and a bag in which to put Medusa's deadly head.

"You haven't got it on properly, Perseus! We can still see your foot," they laughed, as Perseus put on the helmet.

Chapter Five
Medusa

Once the helmet was adjusted, the Ocean Nymphs directed Perseus to where the three Gorgons lived and off he flew, invisible to all. As he grew near, Perseus could hear the rumbling, growling snores of the sisters.

"I must not look down! I must not look down! I must not look down!" he reminded himself.

 He angled his shield and looked into it –
there he beheld a most fearful sight. The three
sisters were sleeping down below him, but even
so, the head of Medusa writhed with dozens
of hissing serpents. Knowing that he must
act before they woke, Perseus fearlessly raised
his sickle high, and with one mighty stroke,
sliced off Medusa's head. He grabbed hold of
a handful of snakes and stuffed them into the
bag as quickly as he could. As he leapt into the
air, one of Medusa's sisters woke.

"Wake up! Wake up! Medusa's lost her head!" she cried.

But Perseus was invisible to all.

"Who's got Medusa's head?" cried the second sister. "Where? How?"

"Fanged if I know," said the first, "but I can't say I'm sorry. All that hissing kept me awake at night."

Chapter Six
Home Again

Perseus's journey home was not an easy one.
It took him over mountains and across stormy
seas; through battles and past monsters, but
finally he arrived back at Seriphos.

"So where's the welcoming committee?"
muttered Perseus as he anchored in the bay
with no one to meet him.

Most people had given him up for dead,
including his poor mother, who he found
in the temple, hiding from King Polydectes

and his unwanted attention.

"Oh, Perseus," she cried with joy, "you're alive! Poly is still trying to force me to marry him. I daren't even put my toes outside the temple."

"Don't worry, Mum," Perseus replied. "Medusa and I will soon sort him out!"

Clutching the bag containing Medusa's head, Perseus rushed to the palace. There, Polydectes was just remarking to his dog how delightful it was to imagine Perseus being turned to stone by Medusa.

"Perseus, as a lump of granite! What a

heavenly thought," he smiled to his dog.

"I'm not so sure," growled the dog, whose keen senses had alerted him to the approach of Perseus.

When Perseus walked in, the king nearly fainted with surprise.

"Wh-wh-why aren't you stone dead?" was all he could think of to say.

"I've returned, just as I promised, with a very special wedding present for you!" and with that, Perseus pulled out Medusa's head

and waved it before the king. Her terrifying gaze immediately turned King Polydectes to stone.

After celebrating the death of the king, Perseus and his mother decided it was time they returned to Argos. Before they left, they crowned Dictys the new King of Seriphos and the whole island turned out to make merry – even Polydectes' dog.

The following day Perseus and his mother

set sail for Argos, where they lived happily ever after. Except for the fact that Perseus, quite accidentally, did kill King Acrisius – just as the oracle had predicted. Which goes to show that you can't avoid your fate, even if you do lock it up in a box and push it out to sea!

Other fabulous retellings by
Marcia Williams

Available from all good booksellers

www.walker.co.uk